FARM CATS

BARNYARD FRIENDS

Jason Cooper

The Rourke Book Co., Inc.
Vero Beach, Florida 32964

Edited by Sandra A. Robinson and Pamela J.P. Schroeder

PHOTO CREDITS
All photos © Lynn M. Stone

DEDICATION
For Brittany and her cat

Library of Congress Cataloging-in-Publication Data

Cooper, Jason, 1942-
    Farm cats / by Jason Cooper.
      p. cm. — (Barn yard friends)
    Includes index.
    ISBN 1-55916-094-2
      1. Cats—Juvenile literature. [1. Cats. 2. Farm life.]
I. Title. II. Series: Cooper, Jason, 1942- Barn yard friends.
SF445.7.C66   1995
636.8'0886—dc20   94-39535
                                                              CIP
                                                              AC

Printed in the USA

TABLE OF CONTENTS

FARM CATS

Farmers don't raise cats as they might raise cattle or corn. However, farmers like to have cats around. **Domestic,** or tame, cats are common animals on thousands of North American farms.

Farm cats have a great deal of freedom to come and go. Many live almost like wild animals.

Farm cats aren't "fancy" like their city cat cousins. They often wear the scars of fights with other cats and wild animals.

Cats love to rub against things, but the Guernsey cow's wet muzzle is a moving target!

HOW CATS LOOK

Like wild cats, domestic cats have long bodies, short jaws and sharp teeth. They also have sharp claws that they can stick out — or pull back into their paws.

Cats have large, bright eyes and long whiskers that help them feel their way through tight spaces.

Domestic cats usually weigh between six and 15 pounds. Farm cats often weigh less than house cats. Farm cats are more active than house cats, and they don't always eat as well.

A cat's curiosity may lead its long body almost anywhere

WHERE CATS LIVE

Pet cats are often kept indoors all the time, or at least at night. Farm cats spend some of their time indoors, too, but not in the farmer's house!

Farm cats prowl around the farm. They explore pastures, gardens, barnyards and barns. They find shelter wherever they can — in places like haylofts and under buildings.

Farm cats are the "top dogs" when it comes to climbing in barn rafters

BREEDS OF CATS

Some domestic cats belong to a special group, or type, of cat — called a **breed.** When a cat belongs to a breed, it looks and acts like others of the same breed. All *Siamese* cats, for example, have a cream-colored body, and dark ears, legs and tail.

Farm cats are not a special breed. They are a mixed breed, or **alley cats.** Farm cats can be mostly yellow, gray, black or white, or a crazy-quilt mixture of colors.

This calico kitten wears a furry quilt of colors

"Darn! Doesn't that milking machine ever leak a few drops?"

"How can I cross someone's path when I'm hiding in this basket?"

WILD CATS

As many as 7,000 years ago, people began to catch and tame the small, wild cats of Africa. They were the first domestic cats.

However, out of the 37 kinds of wild cats, most have never been tamed. Some of these cats — lions, tigers, cheetahs, leopards, lynxes and cougars — live all over the world, except in Antarctica.

The largest wild cats are Siberian tigers. They weigh up to 600 pounds! Tigers, and many other kinds of wild cats, are **endangered.** These cats are in danger of becoming **extinct,** or disappearing forever.

This little cat, a Bengal tiger kitten, will grow up to be a 400-pound cat!

BABY CATS

A mother cat usually has a **litter** of three to five kittens. The mother raises her kittens without any help from the tomcat, or father cat.

Like wild cats, farm cats often hide their babies. Living in an out-of-the-way place helps the mother feel safe.

Newborn kittens cannot see or hear for a few days. By the end of three weeks, the kittens' eyes and ears open, and they begin to explore.

Barn hay is home for this kitten and its mother with the matching fur coat

HOW CATS ARE RAISED

When cats are six months old, most are nearly full-grown. By then, farms cats have learned how to take care of themselves. Most farmers provide cat food, but some farm cats live on what they hunt.

Most farmers don't carefully control the number of cats on their farms. When the farm becomes crowded with cats, the farmer tries to find people who will take kittens home.

This cat wears a sparrow feather on her chin — a trophy of her hunt

HOW CATS ACT

Every cat is a little different. Cats may act friendly toward people, or be very shy. Farm cats are often quick to run away from people. They are shy because they don't see people as often as house cats do.

Like all domestic cats, farm cats spend up to 16 hours each day taking short snoozes — "catnaps." They also take time to **groom** themselves with their rough tongues.

Cats make many sounds when they "talk." They purr, meow, growl, chirp and even yowl.

A farm cat turns a flower box into a mattress for a midday catnap

HOW CATS ARE USED

Cats can be good friends. However, farmers like cats mostly because they kill the mice and rats that live in barns.

Cats are skilled hunters. They leap and climb easily. They can run fast — up to 30 miles per hour.

In the dim light of barns, cats see much better than people do. Cats also have keen hearing and an excellent sense of smell.

Glossary

alley cat (AL lee KAT) — a cat of mixed breeds; a stray or domestic cat living on its own

breed (BREED) — a special group or type of an animal, such as a *Siamese* cat

domestic (dum ES tihk) — referring to any of several kinds of animals tamed and raised by humans

endangered (en DANE jerd) in danger of no longer existing; very rare

extinct (ex TINKT) — no longer existing

groom (GROOM) — to comb and clean hair or fur

litter (LIH ter) — an animal's newborn young, babies